Great Artists
Grandma Moses

ABDO
Publishing Company

Adam G. Klein

visit us at
www.abdopublishing.com

Published by ABDO Publishing Company, 4940 Viking Drive, Edina, Minnesota 55435. Copyright © 2007 by Abdo Consulting Group, Inc. International copyrights reserved in all countries. No part of this book may be reproduced in any form without written permission from the publisher. The Checkerboard Library™ is a trademark and logo of ABDO Publishing Company.

Printed in the United States.

Cover Photo: Corbis
Interior Photos: AP/Wide World pp. 13, 23; Art Resource pp. 15, 27; Corbis pp. 1, 9, 11, 21, 28, 29; Galerie St. Etienne pp. 17, 19, 25; Getty Images pp. 5, 22

Grandma Moses illustrations pp. 9, 15, 17, 19, 25, 27 Copyright © 2006, Grandma Moses Properties Co., New York. Grandma Moses quote p. 15 © 1952 (renewed 1980) Grandma Moses Properties Co., New York.

Series Coordinator: Megan M. Gunderson
Editors: Heidi M. Dahmes, Megan M. Gunderson
Cover Design: Neil Klinepier
Interior Design: Dave Bullen

Library of Congress Cataloging-in-Publication Data

Klein, Adam G., 1976-
  Grandma Moses / Adam G. Klein.
     p. cm. -- (Great artists)
  Includes index.
  ISBN-10 1-59679-737-1
  ISBN-13 978-1-59679-737-6
  1. Moses, Grandma, 1860-1961--Juvenile literature. 2. Painters--United States--Biography--Juvenile literature. 3. Primitivism in art--United States--Juvenile literature. I. Moses, Grandma, 1860-1961. II. Title III. Series: Klein, Adam G., 1976- . Great artists.

  ND237.M78K54 2006
  759.13--dc22
                                                                                         2005017889

Contents

Grandma Moses

Anna Mary Moses is proof that it is never too late to start a new life. She worked on a farm until her late seventies. Then, she became a professional artist known as Grandma Moses. Today, she is considered one of the most important American folk artists ever.

During her years as an artist, Grandma Moses created more than 1,500 paintings. She became an international star and a national celebrity. She continues to have many fans.

Typically, Grandma Moses painted scenes from her community and her life on various farms. At first glance, the paintings seem very simple. The figures appear a bit awkward, and the scenes look flat. But, there is more to these paintings than what is on the surface.

Grandma Moses's art reflects the **unique** experiences she had living and working in small-town America. Her paintings let us look at the world through her eyes. Stare into a Grandma Moses painting and you will wander back in time.

Today, Grandma Moses's works can be found on everything from coffee mugs to magnets.

Timeline

1860 ~ On September 7, Anna Mary Robertson was born in Greenwich, New York.

1887 ~ On November 9, Anna Mary married Thomas Salmon Moses; the couple moved to Staunton, Virginia.

1918 ~ Grandma Moses painted a landscape on a fireboard in her home.

1920 ~ Grandma Moses painted the tip-up table that functioned as her easel.

1927 ~ On January 15, Thomas Salmon Moses died.

1938 ~ Louis J. Caldor discovered Grandma Moses's paintings.

1940 ~ On October 9, Grandma Moses's first solo show opened at the Galerie St. Etienne in New York.

1946 ~ The first set of Grandma Moses Christmas cards were published.

1952 ~ *July Fourth* was donated to the White House; Grandma Moses's autobiography was published.

1955 ~ Edward R. Murrow interviewed Grandma Moses.

1956 ~ *The Eisenhower Farm* was presented to President Eisenhower.

1957 ~ Grandma Moses painted *Lincoln*.

1961 ~ Grandma Moses died on December 13.

Fun Facts

- When Grandma Moses lived in the Shenandoah Valley, she churned butter and made potato chips to help her family earn extra income.

- Soon after their first meeting, Louis J. Caldor sent Grandma Moses some professional painting equipment. He sent more materials after her showing at the Museum of Modern Art.

- One of the many newspaper headlines about Grandma Moses said, "Grandma Moses Just Paints and Makes No Fuss About It." It described her personality very well!

- In 1946, the first book about Grandma Moses was published. It was called *Grandma Moses: American Primitive*.

- When Grandma Moses met with President Harry S. Truman in 1949, she convinced him to play the piano for her while they waited for a storm to pass.

Farm Life

Anna Mary Robertson was born on September 7, 1860, in Greenwich, New York. Her parents were Russell King Robertson and Mary Shannahan. They were **descendants** of Irish and Scottish **immigrants**. Russell, Mary, and their ten children lived and worked on a large farm.

Anna Mary spent her childhood helping her mother take care of her brothers and sisters. Farmwork also kept her busy. So, she did not have a lot of time for school.

In her free time, she enjoyed picking flowers and building rafts with her brothers. With her father's encouragement, Anna Mary also painted a little. But, her mother insisted there were more useful things she should be doing.

One of Anna Mary's earliest memories was from April 1865. She went to town with her aunt and her mother. There, they noticed that the doors and pillars of some of the buildings had

black cloth hanging on them. After learning President Abraham Lincoln had been **assassinated**, Anna Mary's mother became very concerned. That event and her mother's reaction made a big impact on Anna Mary's life.

Grandma Moses painted subjects other than historical events. Often, she focused on daily rural life. **Taking in Laundry** *is just one example of how Grandma Moses concentrated on everyday things in her art.*

Into the World

In 1872, Anna Mary left her home to work. She became a hired girl for a local elderly couple, the Whitesides. At just 12 years old, Anna Mary began cooking, cleaning, sewing, and gardening for them. She also drove the Whitesides to church every Sunday. In return, they treated her like she was their own child.

Anna Mary had lived with them for three years when Mrs. Whiteside passed away. Then, after Mr. Whiteside died, she worked elsewhere as a hired girl until 1887.

On November 9 of that year, Anna Mary married Thomas Salmon Moses. He was a hired man and a farmer. For their honeymoon, the **newlyweds** decided to travel south to North Carolina.

On the way, they stopped in Staunton, Virginia. Local people asked them to settle there. Anna Mary and Thomas liked the beauty of the area. So, they decided to live in the Shenandoah Valley.

Anna Mary and Thomas soon moved onto a 600-acre (243-ha) dairy farm near Fort Defiance, Virginia. There, they raised a

Today, travelers are still attracted to the natural beauty of the Shenandoah Valley.

family. They had ten children, but only five survived. The family worked hard, especially making butter to sell.

The Moses family lived in the Shenandoah Valley until December 1905. That year, they moved north to Eagle Bridge, New York. They bought a farm near Anna Mary's childhood home and continued working in the dairy business.

Early Art

Moses's father had worked on some paintings while he was alive. But due to the demanding amount of farmwork, he rarely had time to paint. As an adult, Moses found herself in a similar situation.

Still, Moses liked to decorate her home. In a school essay, she had written that one of the secrets to happiness is living in a decorated house. She lived her life by this rule. In 1918, Moses painted a landscape on a fireboard, or mantel, in her home.

In 1920, Moses painted a small table that her aunt had given her as a gift. The tip-up table was like an **easel**, so it had a practical function for the artist. This was where Moses would create most of her work.

On January 15, 1927, Thomas Salmon Moses passed away. Moses found it too difficult to take care of the farm by herself. So her son Hugh and his wife, Dorothy, took over much of the farmwork.

The Bennington Museum in Vermont has the largest public collection of Grandma Moses's works. There, visitors can see her tip-up table as well as her art supplies.

But Moses was still full of energy. And, she found herself needing something to fill her time. So, she took up embroidery and began making "worsted pictures," which are pictures made from yarn. These creative projects were just a hint of what was to come.

Folk Art

Moses gave away most of the objects she created to friends and family. But soon, it became difficult for her to sew. Her hands became too sore from the work. Moses's sister Celestia suggested that she try painting instead.

Eventually, Moses would use her bedroom on the farm as her studio. She used the tip-up table that she had decorated in 1920 as her workstation.

Some of the first paintings Moses made were displayed at the Woman's Exchange in Thomas's Drugstore. This was in Hoosick Falls, a town near Eagle Bridge. Moses's paintings hung in the window for all to see.

In 1938, an art collector from New York passed through town. Louis J. Caldor was charmed by the artwork that he saw on display at the drugstore. After finding out who the artist was, Caldor went to visit Moses. Caldor asked if she would paint some pictures for him. She did, and he took them to New York City.

Artist's Corner

Folk art and primitive art are two of the terms used to describe Grandma Moses's style. These art traditions have developed from people who are self-taught. Folk artists usually have little to no professional training. And, they often use unprofessional supplies and materials to create their artwork.

In her autobiography, Grandma Moses wrote that first she would prepare her materials. Then, she would paint "whatever the mind may produce, a landscape, an old bridge, a dream, or a summer or winter scene, childhood memories, but always something pleasing and cheerful." Grandma Moses liked "bright colors and activity."

Deep Snow

Surprise Success

Back in New York City, Caldor refused to give up trying to sell Moses's paintings. Soon, he heard about a show for unknown artists at the Museum of Modern Art (MoMA). The exhibit was called Contemporary Unknown American Painters. Sidney Janis organized the show and accepted three of Moses's paintings.

The Galerie St. Etienne opened in 1939. Caldor heard that the owner, Otto Kallir, was interested in folk art. So, Caldor contacted him. Kallir liked Moses's work.

Kallir allowed Moses to have a solo exhibition in his gallery. What a Farm Wife Painted opened on October 9, 1940, with 34 original works. The day before, a **critic** for the *New York Herald Tribune* reported that Moses's neighbors called her "Grandma Moses." The name stuck.

Moses's first solo exhibition was a success. Only three works sold, but she received public recognition. Several major papers

Repetition

Grandma Moses often painted the same subject many times but in different ways. One subject she painted at least three times is the arrival of an automobile in the quiet countryside.

The First Automobile was included in the MoMA exhibit. In it, the car takes up most of the painting. Automobile, 1913 (below) was painted in 1943. There is more activity in this work. Three children stand to watch the car drive past. And horses shy away, showing that the car is noisy and out of place there.

In the third painting, The Old Automobile, the landscape is even more detailed. But still, the car frightens a horse and people stand to watch the car drive by.

wrote about her work. And, the Gimbels Department Store requested to use the exhibit for their Thanksgiving Festival.

Moses went to New York City for the event. She had spent her life in the country, so she was overwhelmed by all the people she met. But at the Gimbels auditorium, her simple, no-nonsense lifestyle won over the audience. And, she became a celebrity.

Painting History

Grandma Moses was growing in popularity. She received requests for copies of certain paintings. She did not enjoy doing this, but she **reluctantly** gave in to people's requests. Grandma Moses did not want to disappoint her fans, whom she liked to think of as friends.

In a notebook her younger brother Fred had given her, Grandma Moses cataloged her paintings. She put a little printed label on the back of each one. Today, this helps people catalog her works.

Grandma Moses set a fair price for her paintings. She did not like to receive more money than she asked. But because of her growing popularity, Kallir sometimes sold her paintings for more. Grandma Moses didn't understand why people would pay so much and returned the extra money to Kallir.

Grandma Moses loved to create historical paintings. Frequently, the figures she painted repeat from one painting to the next. She often took the figures from history books and old newspaper clippings. But her landscapes are original. And, she portrays animals as they would move in real life. These elements became known as part of her style.

Apple Butter Making *presents another rural scene. People looking to escape to a simpler life connected with scenes like this one.*

Honors

Brundage Greetings Cards produced the first series of Grandma Moses Christmas cards in 1946. It was an easy way for her work to be seen by many people. The 16 designs became very popular. More than 16 million cards were ordered! The next year, Hallmark printed Grandma Moses's Christmas cards.

Grandma Moses's popularity soared. In 1946, her birthday was reported as a news story for the first time. And in 1949, she was honored for her work with the Women's National Press Club Award. President Harry S. Truman gave her the award in front of an impressive crowd.

The next day, Grandma Moses met the Trumans for tea. President Truman found her very charming. A lifelong friendship developed between the two. He never forgot her birthday. And in 1952, her painting *July Fourth* would be donated to the White House. The same painting would become a postage stamp in 1969.

Eventually, Grandma Moses returned to Eagle Bridge. Upon her arrival, cars jammed the road, a high school band played, and schoolchildren sang for her. She had always appreciated the admiration of people all across the country. But, the people at home mattered most to Grandma Moses.

President Truman presented Grandma Moses with an award for her "outstanding accomplishment in Art."

Filling Homes

In 1950, a **documentary** about Grandma Moses was nominated for an **Academy Award**. That same year, Grandma Moses had her first international exhibition. Many new people had the chance to see and appreciate her work. And in 1952, her **autobiography** was published.

When Grandma Moses's friend Helen C. Beers suggested that she decorate **ceramic** tiles, she was thrilled. In one year, she completed 85 tiles. At the age of 91, Grandma Moses still thought it was a great idea to fill a person's home with art. The tiny tiles fit well with this idea.

In 1953, Grandma Moses's life caught the attention of a famous reporter. Edward R. Murrow wanted to interview her for

Grandma Moses was featured on the cover of Time *in December 1953.*

television. He believed that people should see how and where she worked.

Grandma Moses was uncomfortable about the idea at first. She had always felt that a man should not be allowed into her studio because it was in her bedroom. But she was now living in a new house, with a studio just behind the kitchen. So she warmed up to the idea, and the interview took place in 1955.

For the interview, Grandma Moses was filmed painting a whole picture.

Grandma Moses often looked out this window while she painted. ***In*** **Hoosick Valley (from the Window)**, *she even painted the window and curtains around the main scene!*

Then, Murrow interviewed her. She even made him draw a picture! It was a great look into her life and her personality.

A President's Farm

Twenty presidents served the United States during Grandma Moses's lifetime. President Dwight D. Eisenhower was the nineteenth. Eisenhower sometimes painted, and he was a fan of Grandma Moses's work.

To help celebrate Eisenhower's third year as president, Grandma Moses was asked to paint the Eisenhower farm. But she had never seen it. Grandma Moses felt most comfortable painting from her memories. But it was an honor to be asked, and she always wanted to please people. So, she worked from photographs.

The Eisenhower Farm was presented to the president in 1956. Eisenhower felt it had quirkiness and charm. He liked that Grandma Moses had made creative changes to the details of his farm. And, she had captured many of the things he liked most about his farm despite these changes.

Grandma Moses created two paintings for President Eisenhower.
The Eisenhower Home (above) *shows a different view of the
farm than the one that was presented to the president.*

Grandma Moses also continued creating historical paintings.
She painted works based on the **Revolutionary War**, in which
some of her relatives had fought. And in 1957, she painted
Lincoln based on her memory of Lincoln's **assassination**. Even
at the age of 97, her memory was as good as ever. She portrayed
the event as if it had happened the day before.

Turning 100

Grandma Moses turned 100 years old in 1960. In her honor, the governor of New York, Nelson Rockefeller, declared September 7 of that year as Grandma Moses Day. Planning for the grand occasion began in May!

Big events were planned for the celebration. Many people from around the world sent her their best wishes. Grandma Moses's home was open for a week to those who wanted to congratulate her. Many famous people, including several presidents, wanted to honor her.

Grandma Moses did not let her old age stop her from working. She had always been busy, and painting gave her a sense of purpose. In 1960, she was asked to illustrate Clement C. Moore's poem "The Night Before Christmas."

Grandma Moses did not accept the project right away. But since she was familiar with the story, she eventually agreed to do the job. Grandma Moses put her imagination to work. The final book was published after her death and became very popular.

Certain images repeat in each of Grandma Moses's maple sugar works, including someone pouring syrup onto the snow to make candy. Sugaring Off *is just one example of this popular theme in Grandma Moses's works.*

Final Days

Grandma Moses's health was beginning to fail. So, her family moved her into a nursing home in Hoosick Falls. Grandma Moses found it difficult to get used to her new life. For most of her life, she had lived on a farm. And, she had always been very independent. Now, the doctors did not even want her to paint. They thought it would be too hard on her.

Grandma Moses looked forward to returning to her farm and painting again. But on December 13, 1961, Grandma Moses passed away at the age of 101. She was buried in the Hoosick Falls Maple Grove Cemetery next to her husband, her son Hugh, and her daughter Winona. The ceremony was simple, just as she had wanted.

In Eagle Bridge, there is even a street named after Grandma Moses!

The school Grandma Moses attended in Eagle Bridge is now found at the Bennington Museum. There, visitors can view exhibitions on the artist as well as the Murrow documentary.

GRANDMA MOSES SCHOOLHOUSE MUSEUM

DIST. No. 3

In her lifetime, Grandma Moses had about 100 solo shows and 100 group exhibitions. Through her paintings, Grandma Moses welcomes people into her world. She presents visions of the past and hope for the future.

Glossary

Academy Award - an award given by the Academy of Motion Picture Arts and Sciences to the best actors and filmmakers of the year.

assassinate - to murder a very important person, usually for political reasons.

autobiography - a story of a person's life that is written by himself or herself.

ceramic - of or relating to a nonmetallic product, such as pottery or porcelain.

critic - a professional who gives his or her opinion on art or performances.

descendant - a person who comes from a particular ancestor or group of ancestors.

documentary - a film or television program that presents facts, often about an event or a person.

easel - a stand that holds a painter's canvas.

immigrate - to enter another country to live. A person who immigrates is called an immigrant.

newlywed - a person who just married.

reluctant - feeling unwilling or hesitant to do something.

Revolutionary War - from 1775 to 1783. A war for independence between Britain and its North American colonies. The colonists won and created the United States of America.

unique - being the only one of its kind.

Saying It

ceramic - suh-RA-mihk

Galerie St. Etienne - GA-luh-ree SAYNT eh-TYEHN

Otto Kallir - AW-toh kuh-LEER

Shenandoah Valley - sheh-nuhn-DOH-uh VA-lee

Web Sites

To learn more about Grandma Moses, visit ABDO Publishing Company on the World Wide Web at **www.abdopub.com**. Web sites about Grandma Moses are featured on our Book Links page. These links are routinely monitored and updated to provide the most current information available.

Index